C000127643

1 MONTH OF
FREE
READING

at
www.ForgottenBooks.com

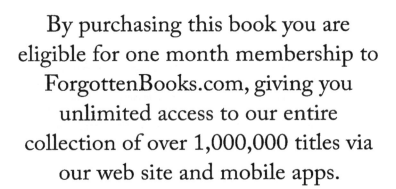

By purchasing this book you are eligible for one month membership to ForgottenBooks.com, giving you unlimited access to our entire collection of over 1,000,000 titles via our web site and mobile apps.

To claim your free month visit: www.forgottenbooks.com/free1115280

ISBN 978-0-331-38235-8
PIBN 11115280

vc

THE

Cotton

SITUATION

FOR RELEASE
APR. 19, P. M.

BUREAU OF AGRICULTURAL ECONOMICS
UNITED STATES DEPARTMENT OF AGRICULTURE

CS-127   BAE   JAN.- FEB.- MAR 1950

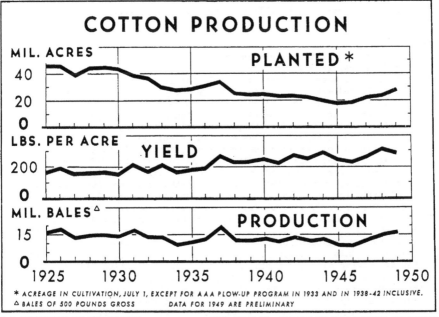

COTTON PRODUCTION

* ACREAGE IN CULTIVATION, JULY 1, EXCEPT FOR AAA PLOW-UP PROGRAM IN 1933 AND IN 1938-42 INCLUSIVE.
△ BALES OF 500 POUNDS GROSS   DATA FOR 1949 ARE PRELIMINARY

U S DEPARTMENT OF AGRICULTURE   NEG 47496-XX   BUREAU OF AGRICULTURAL ECONOMICS

Substantial reductions in cotton acreage during the last quarter century have been largely offset by increases in per acre yields. Consequently, annual production of cotton is only moderately lower. The cotton acreage in 1949 was 40 percent below that in 1925, but the dif- in total production for the two years was only one percent. Yields per acre have increased by about two-thirds during the last 25 years. Current high yields have been possible through increased use of fertilizer, more effective insect control, use of improved seed and cultural practices, selection of land better adapted to cotton, and shift in acreage from low to higher yielding areas.

CONTENTS

- - - - - - - - - - - - - - - - - - - -
T H E   C O T T O N   S I T U A T I O N
- - - - - - - - - - - - - - - - - - - -

Approved by the Outlook and Situation Board, April 6, 1950

SUMMARY

Public Law 471, 81st Congress, 2nd session, amends the Agricultural Adjustment Act of 1938, as amended, to provide for an increase to the initial National cotton acreage allotment of 21,000,000 acres. The extent of the increase will not be known, however, until individual farm adjustments provided by the amendments have been determined.

Spot prices in late March were about 2/3 of a cent per pound below the peak reached in late February. Middling 15/16 inch cotton on March 20 averaged 31.90 cents per pound in the ten spot markets, 0.4 cents per pound higher than at the beginning of the season.

The 1949-50 supply of cotton in the United States is now estimated at 21.4 million bales, 20 percent higher than last season, but only slightly higher than the 1935-39 average.

So far in 1949-50, domestic mill consumption has been higher than in the previous season. It is expected that this relatively high rate will not be maintained during the remaining 5 months (March-July), but the total will be around 8.5 million bales for the full 1949-50 season, compared with 7.8 million bales in 1948-49.

Prospective exports of raw cotton in 1949-50 are nearly around 5-1/4 million bales (including 300,000 bales for India and 125,000 for Communist China). In 1948-49, exports were 4-3/4 million bales.

The carry-over on August 1, 1950 (beginning of next season) is likely to be around 7.5 million bales of which about two-thirds will be in CCC stocks. The carry-over of low grade cotton is expected to be relatively small, and most of the carry-over of the better cottons probably will be in the CCC stocks.

U. S. exports of cotton textiles have declined in recent months and an adjustment to a new level, lower than in preceding postwar years, appears to be a possibility.

National Cotton Acreage Allotment
    Increased by Public Law 471.

        The provisions of Public Law 471, 81st Congress, 2nd session
which amends the Agricultural Act of 1938, as amended, increases the
initial National Allotment of 21 million acres for the 1950 crop. The
extent of the increase, in terms of acres, will not be known until later.
Public Law 471 provides for establishment in 1950 of minimum farm cotton
acreage allotments, upon application by the owner or operator, equal to
the larger of (a) 65 percent of the average acreage, or (b) 45 percent
of the highest acreage, during three years 1946, 1947, and 1948, which
was planted to cotton or regarded as planted to cotton under Public
Law 12, 79th Congress (which allows credit for cotton acreage shifted
to war crops), with a maximum limitation on the increase of 40 percent
of the cropland of the farm. The additional acreage is to be in addition to the county, State, and national acreage allotments already pro-
claimed for 1950, but is not to be taken into account in establishing
future acreage allotments. Authorizes the reallotment in 1950 to farms
in the same county, to the extent necessary to provide the allotments
authorized by this Act, of any acreage alloted to individual farms which
will not be planted to cotton and is voluntarily surrendered to the county
committee. If any acreage remains after such allotments, it may be appor-
tioned to other farms in the same county were allotments are determined
to be inadequate. In subsequent years the acreage surrendered and re-
allocated shall be credited to the State and county. Section 2 of the
Act provides that any farmer who is dissatisfied with his cotton acreage allotment for 1950 may apply for a review.

        The extent to which farmers will utilize or voluntarily return
to the County Committee any unused portion of an allotment can not be
estimated. However, data are available on the utilization of allotments
for the crops 1938-1943, previous years when marketing quotas were in
effect. As shown in table 3, the planted acreage ranged from 91 percent
of the allotted acreage in 1938 to 80 percent in 1943, based on a national allotment of 27 million acres.

Prices Moderately Above Loan Rate

        In late March, prices for cotton had declined somewhat from the
peak prices for the current season which were reached in February.
Prices for Middling 15/16 inch cotton averaged 31.90 cents per pound in
the ten spot markets on March 20 compared with 32.51 cents on February 25
(peak so far this season), and 32.67 cents a year earlier. The March 20
price was as shown in table 4, 1.1 percent above the 10 spot market price
on August 1, 1949 (beginning of season).

        Some qualities of cotton have advanced during most of the season
and are substantially above the loan rate due to a shortage of those qualities in the carry-over on August 1, 1949, the low production of these grades
in the 1949 crop, and a heavy demand for these grades during the entire season both for export and domestic mill use. The 1949-50 season opened with
only 1.5 million bales of "free" cotton. Such stocks were less than a two-
months supply at the June-July 1949 rate of disappearance, assuming that
the grade and staple length distribution, was in balance with requirements.
The remaining 3.8 million bales in the August 1 carry-over were in the CCC
pool and for all practical purposes were not available to the trade. With

such small "free" stocks, the mills were generally short of cotton when
the sudden improvement in the demand for gray cloth occurred in late July
and early August. With the grade distribution of the 1949 crop, diffi-
culty has been experienced in obtaining and maintaining sufficient stocks
of cotton in certain grades.

Prices received by farmers for cotton averaged 28.05 cents per
pound in mid-March. This compared with 27.50 cents in February and
28.74 cents a year ago. The increase from the February level places the
March index of cotton prices at 236 percent of the 1910-14 average. The
March index was 93 percent of parity compared with 92 percent a month
earlier and 94 percent a year ago. The effective parity price for cotton on March 15 was 30.01 cents per pound, 0.13 cents above a month err-
lier and only one percent below a year ago.

1949 Crop--15.9 Million Bales
1949-50 Supply--21.4 Million Bales

The 1949-50 cotton marketing season opened with a carry-over of
5.3 million bales of which 3.8 million bales, or 72 percent, was loan
cotton pooled for the producers' account by the Commodity Credit Corporation on August 1, 1949. The 1949 cotton crop was the sixth largest on
record and produced 15.9 million running bales. Including an estimate
of 175,000 bales for imports and assuming that pre-season ginnings from
the 1950 crop balance those in the previous crop, brings the total supply of cotton in the United States during the current season to 21.4 million bales, compared with 17.8 million last season and the 1935-39 average
of 21.3 million.

Despite the large crop in 1949, production of most of the highest
and lowest grades of cotton was relatively short. The weather during the
harvesting season was primarily responsible for the distribution in grades.
Rainy weather during the early part of the harvesting season lowered the
grade of the early crop which normally supplies the better grades. Un-
usually favorable weather in the late harvesting season held up the grade
of the late crop, which normally supplies most of the lower grades. The
result was, as shown in table 6, a concentration of cotton in the medium
white grades and the spotted and grey cottons and a smaller crop of the
highest and lowest grades as compared with the 1948 crop.

In 1949, Oklahoma, Texas and the three western cotton producing
States—Arizona, California, and New Mexico—produced over half the crop.
This is the second time in history and the first time since 1923 when
heavy boll weevil infestation cut the eastern crop to less than half the
total that this has occurred. Texas ginned 5,860,000 bales, or 37 percent of the crop, while ginnings in the other four States totaled
2,680,000 bales, or 17 percent. Table 7 shows acreage harvested and ginnings, by States, for each of the last three crops. Between 1947 and 1949,
there was a total increase in acreage harvested of about 5,600,000 acres,
of which the five western States accounted for 59 percent. However, because of favorable weather, these States accounted for 88 percent of the
total U. S. increase in 1949 of 4,344,000 running bales over 1947. Unfavorable weather and heavy boll weevil infestation in the central and
southeastern cotton States reduced yields in 1949 by 32 percent from the
all-time high average yield of 396 pounds per acre in 1948.

Domestic Mill Consumption
8.5 Million Bales

The use of cotton by domestic mills in the first seven months of the current season was 5,079,000 bales. This was 5 percent more than a year ago and 26 percent more than the average for the corresponding months in 1935-39. The trend of mill consumption has been sharply upward since the beginning of the season. The January-February average daily mill use of cotton, adjusted for seasonal, was 29 percent above the extremely low level of June-July last year and, at a daily rate of over 35,000 bales, was at an annual rate of nearly 9,000,000 bales. If mill use of cotton in the five remaining months of the current season is at the adjusted January-February rate, total domestic mill consumption for the current season would be 8.9 million bales, 1.1 million bales or 14 percent above last season.

However, some unfavorable developments affecting future mill activity are in evidence, and the prospect is that mill use of cotton during the March-July period will decline more than seasonal. If so, the aggregate for these five months will not be more than 3.5 million bales. Domestic mill consumption for the entire 1949-50 season in this event, would total around 8.5 million bales.

Retail sales of textiles through February recovered somewhat from the low levels of last summer, but they were still running below a year ago. In addition, pre-Easter sales of apparel were unexpectedly slow in early March, partly resulting in some price weakness for many constructions. Exports of cotton cloth are at the lowest level since 1944 with no indication of any substantial or sustained increase. Imports of cotton cloth, although insignificant as compared with the total domestic cloth production, are increasing and may be higher this season than in any preceding postwar year. In view of these developments, therefore, it is likely that demands on the mills for gray cloth will decline more than seasonally during the remainder of the season.

Cotton prices in the ten spot markets, with the exception of some of the medium qualities which are in large supply, are 2 or more cents per pound above the corresponding loan rate. Because cotton prices increased more than gray cloth prices, gross mill margins on 17 selected constructions declined slightly in both January and February. Recently, secondhand goods appeared on the market at somewhat less than going prices. With little change in the price of cotton from February, mill margins narrowed again in March. With raw material costs rising in relation to selling prices and the average loan rate likely to be lower next season, it is unlikely that mills will produce substantial quantities of cloth for inventory.

Exports of Raw Cotton Expected To
Exceed 5-1/4 Million Bales.

Exports of U. S. cotton in the first seven months of the 1949-50 season were substantially above the comparable period for any season since 1939-40, when war stock-piling and an export subsidy increased the volume of foreign takings of U. S. cotton.

For the August-February period of the current season, U. S. exports totaled 3,068,000 bales (tables 10 and 16). For the corresponding period last season, 2,382,000 bales had been exported, compared with 4,917,000 bales in 1939-40. Significant increases in the volume to France, Japan, United Kingdom, Germany and Netherlands, have been largely responsible for exports during the current season exceeding last season by 29 percent. Spectacular increases, percentage-wise, but of lesser importance in volume were made in shipments to Greece, Hungary, Spain, and Cuba.

Direct financing by the U. S. Government has accounted for a large proportion of all exports of U. S. cotton since the war. In the August-February period of the current season, exports to those European countries participating in the ECA cotton program were slightly over 2,015,000 bales two thirds of total exports while those to Japan and Korea were 428,000 bales, or 14 percent of the total of 3.1 million bales. As of April 1, 1950, ECA had issued purchase authorizations for U. S. cotton to be exported during the fiscal year 1949-50, totaling slightly over 565 million dollars, of which 10.4 million was to Korea. Such authorizations, (nearly 90 million dollars of which were issued in the previous fiscal year, but all of which provide for shipment during the current fiscal year) would cover about 3.6 million bales or nearly two-thirds of the estimated exports in the 1949-50 fiscal year. Table 11 shows the distribution of these purchase authorizations by country of destination.

The prospect is that exports in the last five months of the current season (March-July) will be at a higher rate than during the first seven months and will total around 2-1/4 million running bales. If so, the full season total will exceed 5-1/4 million running bales. India has set aside exchange and authorized import licenses to import 300,000 bales of U. S. cotton during the second half of the current season while Communist-China will attempt to import 125,000 bales. Even if neither of these plans materializes, the total volume of U. S. cotton exports in 1949-50 may reach 5.0 million bales and exceed last season by about 300,000 bales.

In the March-July period, exports to Europe, including United Kingdom and Russia, may be at a higher level than during the first seven months and total about 1.6 million bales. Exports to Africa, Oceania, Central and South America should be about 70,000 bales, or about the same rate as during the August-February period. Procurement of cotton from Mexico by Canada has been heavy and may mean that exports of U. S. cotton to Canada during March-July will be substantially less than in the first seven months. Expected increases in the level of exports to India, Communist-China, Japan and Korea would bring the total exports to Asia during the last five months to over 600,000 bales nearly equal to that for the first seven months.

Carry-over August 1, 1950--
Around 7.5 Million Bales

The supply in 1949-50 is estimated at 21.4 million bales. If domestic mill consumption approximates 8.5 million bales as expected, and exports are around 5-1/4 million bales, total disappearance for the full season will be about 13-3/4 million bales. This would indicate that cotton stocks at the end of the current season are likely to be around 7.5 million bales.

CCC Loan Stocks On August 1, 1950
Probably About 5 Million Bales

About two-thirds of the end of season stocks are expected to be
Commodity Credit Corporation loan and pooled cotton. "Free" stocks are
likely to be higher than the 1.5 million bales of a year earlier but
the actual increase depends largely on prospects in the late months of
the current season as to the 1950-51 loan rate, the size and quality of
1950 crop, and the demand for cotton for use by domestic mills and for
export in the early part of the next season. It is expected that CCC
stocks will be about 5.0 million bales.

As of March 30, reported CCC loans on 1949 crop cotton were only
3,160,000 bales of which 767,000 had been redeemed. For the four weeks
ending March 30, only 45,000 bales were placed under loan while
377,000 bales were redeemed. The low level of loans and high level of
repayments reported during these four weeks is largely due to the relatively high prices during this period. In the ten spot markets, Middling
15/16 inch cotton averaged over 2 cents per pound, or nearly 10 percent,
above the equivalent loan rate. Prices of many other qualitites of cotton, particularly those of Low Middling white or lower grades, were even
more favorable relative to the loan rate.

During the heavy harvesting months, prices for cotton were not as
high as during March. However, since early in the season the strong
demand for cotton both for use by domestic mills and for export, coupled
with small "free" stocks on August 1, 1949 and the grade distribution in
the 1949 crop, has generally maintained prices sufficiently above the
loan rate to hold entries into the Government loan to a low level. ECA
policy requires that a specified portion of all cotton procured with
ECA funds be Low Middling or lower grades and consequently has kept this
kind of cotton moving into trade channels. The exact proportion of total
procurement (exports) of cotton that must be in the low grades varies
from country to country, depending on condition of mill machinery and
equipment, composition of prewar exports of U. S. cotton as to grades,
market outlets for the textiles, etc. but ranges from 12-1/2 percent for
Great Britain to 17-1/2 percent for Germany.

Cotton can be placed under loan until April 30 and redeemed from
the loan until August 1. There are several considerations that will affect
the volume of cotton that will be placed under or redeemed from the loan
before the end of the season. ECA purchase authorizations for cotton in
late March totalled 74 million dollars, (nearly 500,000 bales). Since
this cotton must be exported by June 15, 1950, a moderate demand can be
expected for cotton for the remainder of the season. The price of cotton has not declined substantially in recent weeks from the season's
high level reached in late February. The loan rate on Middling 7/8 inch
for 1950 crop cotton, average location, seems likely to be slightly lower
than during the current season. Barring unforeseen economic declines or
other international disruptions, world mill consumption and U. S. exports
of cotton in 1950-51 may be about the same as in the current season.
Farmers' intentions to plant cotton are not officially forecast but the
initial national allotment in 1950 of 21 million acres was increased
some by subsequent legislation.

On balance, it appears that CCC loans for 1949 crop cotton will not exceed 3-1/4 million bales, a large part of which will be redeemed by the producer. CCC stocks of cotton at the beginning of the 1950-51 season are expected to be about 5.0 million bales including the pooled cotton from the 1948 crop.

Exports of Cotton
Textiles Decline

Changes in the volume of cotton cloth exported from the U. S. in recent months indicate a severe downward adjustment. This declining trend may mean that a lower level of exports is in the making and that the United States will no longer hold the position as chief supplier to the world textile markets which it held in the immediate postwar years.

In 1947, U. S. exports of cotton cloth were nearly 1.5 billion square yards and accounted for 15 percent of the total domestic production of cotton cloth. This volume--five times as high as 1930-39 average-- now stands as an all-time peak for U. S. exports of cotton cloth. In 1948, exports declined to 940 million square yards and comprised about 10 percent of domestic cotton textile output. In the first ten months of 1949 exports were approximately at the same level as for the corresponding period in 1948, but a drop in volume in both November and December held the full year's total down to 880.2 million square yards.

The decline in exports from 1947 to 1949 partially indicates the recovery from war damage of the textile industry in Europe and Japan. In 1947, Europe and Great Britain were wrestling with problems such as rebuilding an adequate skilled mill force, procurement of sufficient supplies of desirable cotton, repair and modernization of mill plants and equipment, and exchange difficulties. Under such conditions, these important prewar textile exporting countries could not compete with U. S. mills, either from the standpoint of cost or production. Japanese mills were under rigid regulations and were not allowed to operate more than 2-1/4 million spindles (about 20 percent of prewar) and could export cloth only at prices comparable to U. S. prices. Consequently, during 1947, cotton cloth was exported from the United States to a substantially larger number of countries than prewar. Many of these new customers were normal markets for European, United Kingdom or Japanese products. Analysis of tables 13 and 14 indicate that the aggregate exports of U. S. cotton cloth in 1939 to countries taking 15 million square yards or more comprised 81 percent of total exports, while in 1947 with exports more widespread as to the number of countries, aggregate exports of countries taking 15 million square yards or more accounted for only 55 percent of total cloth exports.

In 1948 and 1949, European and British mills, with the assistance of U. S. government financed cotton, were largely successful in reaching postwar goals (for some countries these were above prewar levels) in volume of production of cotton cloth. In Japan, textile export regulations were gradually relaxed and in late 1949 were practically lifted. While the cotton cloth produced in these and other countries (notably India, where the 1950 goal for cloth exports is nearly one

billion yards) was becoming more competitive with U. S. goods in the world
textile markets, the dollar exchange situation in many textile importing
countries was deteriorating and partially or wholly effective barriers
were erected against the importation of U. S. textiles. The Philippine
Republic, historically the second largest single offshore outlet, has
limited imports of U. S. cloth during 1950 to 25 percent of the 1948
volume. Jamaica no longer is taking any U. S. goods. Postwar expansions
of cloth production in other prewar mainstay markets, such as Cuba, Canada
and South America, has also limited exports recently. As a consequence,
U. S. exports of cotton textiles declined in late 1949, not only in total
volume but also as to number of countries.

In January 1950, exports dropped below 40 million square yards for
the first time in six years. Although nearly two-thirds higher than the
1935-39 average, these exports were only 36.5 million square yards, compared with 55.9 million in December and 102.3 million in the preceding
January. If January should be typical for the year, the 1950 total would
be the lowest since before the war.

A substantial reduction in annual cotton textile exports from 1948
and 1949 levels would probably affect domestic mills more adversely than
the offsetting reduction in cloth production would indicate. Certainly
the large volume of textile exports in 1947 delayed the dangerous opera-
tion of curtailing cloth production and of reducing cloth prices. A
still large export market acted as a sedative when it did happen during
1948 and the first half of 1949. It is improbable that this re-adjustment,
which as a whole was orderly and without mishap, could have been accom-
plished without substantial disruptions had there not been such large exports to serve as a cushion.

Whether the downward trend in current exports really portends a
permanent lower level is problematical and depends, in large measure,
on the combined effects of several factors, over most of which the domestic mills have no control. Some of the factors that will determine the
subsequent volume of U. S. cotton textile exports are the general economic
conditions in the importing countries, the actions by the governments of
these countries as to import restrictions against U. S. goods, which, in
turn, may depend on the extent to which trade can be established or re-
established with the United States in other items, the ultimate result of
the devaluation of currencies, the extent to which the textile industry
in Europe and Japan eventually recovers, which, in turn, depends largely
on the future ability of these countries to procure cotton through their
own resources, the extent to which both foreign textile importing and exporting countries substitute rayon and other synthetics, including paper,
plastics, etc., to fill the gap in cotton textile requirements, and the
extent to which textile production becomes the nucleus industry in the
several nations which now are industrializing their economy for the first
time. Other important factors--and over these the domestic mills can
exercise control--are merchandising methods and the prices and quality
of U. S. goods.

The world shortage of textiles is large. Excluding the United States, the world population in 1949, at about 2-1/4 billion persons, was 10 percent more than the 1934-38 average, while foreign consumption of cotton in 1949, at about 20.5 million bales, was over 20 percent less than the 1934-38 average. Foreign production of rayon in 1949 was about 1.7 billion pounds or 52 percent more than the 1934-38 average, but this increase which is about equivalent to 1.4 million bales of cotton, falls far short of balancing the reduced consumption in cotton. The combined per capita production of rayon and cotton textiles in all foreign countries in 1949 was about 5.1 pounds, 18 percent less than in 1934-38.

Foreign Production--
  14-3/4 Million Bales

Foreign production of cotton in 1949-50 is expected to be about 14,750,000 American size bales, an increase over the preceding season of 4 percent, but 20 percent below the prewar average. Foreign cotton acreage during the current season is estimated to be nearly 6 percent more than the 40,600,000 acres in 1948-49 but unfavorable weather and heavy insect infestation in the higher yielding areas resulted in a slight reduction in the average yield.

The most substantial increases in foreign production in 1949-50 were made by Mexico and Turkey. A 37 percent acreage increase (about 300,000 acres) in Mexico plus favorable weather resulted in a 1949 crop of about 965,000 bales, 72 percent above 1948. Cotton production in Mexico has been stimulated by the expansion of irrigation facilities in the principal cotton growing areas and the devaluation of the peso in 1948, which increased prices for cotton by 43 percent in terms of Mexican currency. A record cotton crop in 1949 is also indicated for Turkey. The latest crop estimate is 435,000 bales, which would represent an increase above last year of about 125,000 bales or 41 percent.

The cotton acreage in Pakistan is not considered to have changed from the 2.7 million of the previous year but the crop, due to increased yields, is estimated to be 900,000 bales, slightly higher than last year. An increase in acreage of about 10 percent with some improvement over last year in yields is expected to bring the current crop in India up to about 2.3 million bales, 19 percent higher than a year ago. The Brazilian crop in 1949-50 is tentatively estimated at 1,700,000 bales, a substantial increase over last year's crop of 1,540,000 bales. The 1949-50 acreage is expected to be about 500,000 acres more than last year's total of 4.7 million acres.

A sharp drop in 1949 yields, due to severe leafworm and boll worm damage is responsible for a smaller crop in Egypt. At 1.7 million bales, the 1949-50 crop is expected to be 8 percent less than in the previous year, although the cotton acreage, at 1,754,000 acres, is 17 percent above that in 1948-49. The insect damage was generally confined to the area that produces extra long staple cotton.

Table 1.- Cotton: Acreage planted, yield per acre and production,
United States, 1925-49

Year beginning August 1		Acreage in cultivation July 1		Yield per planted acre		Production
	:		:		:	1,000 bales 500 lb. gross
	:	1,000 acres		Pounds		weight
1925		45,968		167.5		16,105
1926		45,839		187.7		17,978
1927		39,471		157.1		12,956
1928	:	43,737		158.4		14,477
1929	:	44,448		159.7		14,825
1930	:	43,329		153.9		13,932
1931		39,110		209.3		17,097
1932		36,494		170.6		13,003
1933	:	1/ 29,753		210.1		13,047
1934		27,860		165.5		9,636
1935	:	28,063		181.5		10,638
1936		30,627		193.8		12,399
1937		34,090		266.2		18,946
1938	:	1/ 24,593		232.5		11,943
1939	:	1/ 24,250		233.5		11,817
1940	:	1/ 24,299		248.0		12,566
1941	:	1/ 22,696		227.2		10,744
1942	:	1/ 22,954		268.2		12,817
1943		21,900		250.1		11,427
1944		19,990		288.5		12,230
1945		17,562		246.3		9,015
1946		18,190		227.4		8,640
1947		21,500		263.7		11,857
1948	:	23,163		307.9		14,877
1949 2/	:	27,359		281.0		16,034

Compiled from records of the Crop Reporting Board.

1/ Excludes for 1933 the 10,495,000 acres plowed up under the AAA program and for 1938 to 1942, inclusive, such acreage as were plowed up in order to conform with farm acreage allotments. These acreages were: 1938--425,000 acres; 1939--433,000 acres; 1940--572,000 acres; 1941--434,000 acres; 1942--348,000.
2/ Forecast as of December 1, 1949.

Table 2.- Cotton: 1950 acreage allotment compared with 1949 acreage

State	1950 acreage allotment 1/	Acreage in cultivation July 1, 1949 2/	Estimated harvested acreage 2/
	1,000 acres	1,000 acres	1,000 acres
Missouri	463	601	583
Virginia	28	33	32
North Carolina	723	822	815
South Carolina	1,026	1,282	1,270
Georgia	1,411	1,567	1,550
Florida	42	46	44
Tennessee	704	845	830
Alabama	1,571	1,825	1,810
Mississippi	2,296	2,885	2,770
Arkansas	1,921	2,534	2,450
Louisiana	873	1,087	1,060
Okl. homa	1,243	1,344	1,300
Texas	7,637	10,811	10,725
New Mexico	170	320	310
Arizona	232	374	373
California	643	983	957
Other States	17	20	19
United States	21,000	27,359	26,898

Compiled from reports of the Crop Reporting Board, PMA.

1/ Not applicable to cotton 1½ inches or more in staple length as provided for in Section 347 of Public Law 272, 81st. Congress.
2/ Estimates as of December 1, 1949.

Table 3.- Cotton: Allotted acreage, planted acreage and percent planted were of allotted, by States and United States, 1938-43 1/

State	Acres allotted 2/						Acres planted 3/						Planted as a percentage of allotted					
	1938	1939	1940	1941	1942	1943	1938	1939	1940	1941	1942	1943	1938	1939	1940	1941	1942	1943
	1,000 acres	1,000 acres	1,000 acres	1,000 acres	1,000 acres	1,000 acres	1,000 acres	1,000 acres	1,000 acres	1,000 acres	1,000 acres	1,000 acres	Per-cent	Per-cent	Per-cent	Per-cent	Per-cent	Per-cent
Missouri	388	396	403	405	409	417	362	380	414	419	426	375	93.3	96.0	102.7	103.5	104.2	89.9
Virginia	57	59	58	57	56	55	42	33	33	36	41	34	73.7	55.9	56.9	63.2	73.2	61.8
North Carolina ..	999	992	995	987	979	983	884	754	841	811	861	850	88.5	76.0	84.5	82.2	87.9	86.5
South Carolina ..	1,371	1,367	1,366	1,356	1,352	1,348	1,263	1,248	1,267	1,232	1,153	1,148	92.1	91.3	92.8	90.9	85.3	85.2
Georgia	2,172	2,270	2,272	2,253	2,240	2,212	2,048	1,982	1,970	1,849	1,734	1,618	94.3	87.3	86.7	82.1	77.4	77.1
Florida	84	90	88	85	84	83	67	64	58	50	56	44	79.8	71.1	65.9	58.8	66.7	53.0
Tennessee	822	832	814	803	801	807	742	753	729	690	725	723	90.3	88.1	89.6	85.9	90.5	89.6
Alabama	2,246	2,308	2,290	2,278	2,259	2,249	2,079	2,099	2,037	1,791	1,722	1,627	92.6	90.9	89.0	78.6	76.2	72.3
Mississippi	2,671	2,707	2,703	2,695	2,673	2,680	2,622	2,661	2,657	2,458	2,438	2,515	98.2	98.3	98.2	91.2	91.2	93.8
Arkansas	2,391	2,394	2,293	2,298	2,290	2,298	2,165	2,187	2,159	2,086	2,021	1,888	90.5	91.4	94.2	90.8	88.3	82.2
Louisiana	1,247	1,269	1,272	1,268	1,258	1,240	1,140	1,153	1,197	1,071	1,028	1,025	91.4	90.9	94.1	84.5	81.7	82.7
Oklahoma	2,287	2,299	2,250	2,214	2,201	2,193	1,733	1,855	1,900	1,733	1,872	1,554	75.8	80.7	84.4	78.2	85.1	70.9
Texas	10,020	10,150	10,003	9,962	9,933	9,897	9,163	8,873	8,869	8,101	8,395	7,889	91.4	87.4	85.7	81.3	84.5	79.7
New Mexico	112	116	118	118	118	120	97	96	108	101	106	93	86.6	82.8	91.5	85.6	89.8	77.5
Arizona	198	191	194	194	194	194	159	148	156	153	144	108	80.3	77.5	80.4	78.9	74.2	55.7
California	402	396	397	400	405	400	356	334	356	356	359	290	88.6	84.3	89.7	89.0	88.6	72.5
Other States 4/ ..	25	27	27	26	26	27	21	21	22	20	22	18	84.0	77.8	81.5	76.9	84.6	66.7
United States 5/16/	27,493	27,863	27,545	27,399	27,280	27,203	24,943	24,622	24,772	22,956	23,103	21,798	90.7	88.4	89.9	83.8	84.7	80.1

Compiled from records of Crop Reporting Board and Agricultural Adjustment Administration.

Grade	10 markets March 20, 1950 Cents	is of Price Aug. 1, 1949 Percent	is of Equivalent loan rate Percent	10 markets March 20, 1950 Cents	is of Price Aug. 1, 1949 Percent	is of Equivalent loan rate Percent	10 markets March 20, 1950 Cents	is of Price Aug. 1, 1949 Percent	is of Equivalent loan rate Percent	10 markets March 20, 1950 Cents	is of Price Aug. 1, 1949 Percent	is of Equivalent loan rate Percent
White												
GM	31.13	103.4	19	32.78	102.3	109.0	34.02	104.3	110.9	34.73	104.6	110.7
SM	31.01	101.5	19	32.67	102.3	109.2	33.90	104.3	110.9	34.62	104.7	0.9
M	30.40	102.4	11	31.90	101.1	107.9	32.93	102.8	091	33.53	103.3	109.1
SLM	27.78	98.3	107.4	28.82	97.9	103.2	29.30	98.6	103.3	29.70	98.8	102.9
LM	25.45	103.9	116.9	26.42	103.8	112.3	26.61	104.3	112.2	26.68	104.6	112.2
SGD	23.56	112.8	133.7	24.51	112.2	125.2	24.74	113.2	261	24.74	113.2	125.5
GO	21.94	118.1	142.3	22.84	116.1	132.3	23.06	117.2	133.5	23.06	117.2	132.0
Spotted												
GM	29.20	102.5	110.7	30.84	101.4	107.9	31.14	101.2	107.7	31.32	100.8	107.2
M	27.03	101.8	110.7	28.55	100.3	107.3	28.80	99.9	106.8	28.92	001	106.4
LM	22.19	119.5	143.9	23.19	115.4	133.1	23.31	116.0	133.8	23.31	115.8	133.4
Tinged												
M	23.63	117.0	136.0	24.60	115.2	129.0	24.71	114.2	128.6	24.71	113.1	127.9
Stained												
SM	22.06	116.5	134.8	23.16	112.8	127.1	23.26	112.9	127.3	23.26	112.8	126.6
Gray												
SM	27.26	104.2	110.5	28.81	102.9	108.2	29.03	102.5	108.0	29.09	102.1	107.3

Computed from data from Cotton Branch, FMA.

Table 5.- Average price for cotton received by farmers, ten spot market average price for Middling 15/16 inch and for Middling 7/8 inch, parity price for cotton and loan rate on Middling 15/16 inch, United States, by years, 1939-48, and by months, 1948 and 1949

Month and year	Average price received by farmers for cotton : Cents	Ten spot markets M 15/16" : Cents	Ten spot markets M 7/8" : Cents	Farm price as percent of ten spot markets M 15/16" : Percent	Farm price as percent of ten spot markets M 7/8" : Percent	Parity price of cotton : Cents	Farm price as percent of 1/ of parity price : Percent	Loan rate on Middling 7/8" : Cents	Farm price as percent of loan rate on M 7/8" : Percent
1939	9.09	0.09	9.90	90.1	91.8	15.38	59.1	8.70	104.5
1940	9.89	.00	10.79	89.9	91.7	15.62	63.3	8.90	1
1941	17.03	18.31	17.94	93.0	94.9	17.73	96.0	14.02	121.5
1942	19.04	20.14	9.2	94.5	99.1	9.2	99.1	7.02	111.9
1943	19.88	20.65	19.56	96.3	101.6	20.58	96.6	18.41	108.0
1944	20.73	21.86	20.60	94.8	100.6	20.96	98.9	20.03	103.5
1945	22.52	25.96	24.39	86.8	92.3	.27	102.0	19.84	113.5
1946	32.64	34.82	33.33	93.7	97.9	26.78	121.9	22.83	143.0
1947	31.93	34.58	32.38	92.3	98.6	30.26	105.5	26.49	120.5
1948									
Aug.	30.41	31.31	28.42	97.1	107.0	30.88	98.5	28.79	105.6
Sept.	30.94	31.18	28.77	99.2	107.5	30.88	100.2	28.79	107.5
Oct.	31.08	31.21	28.91	99.6	107.5	30.63	101.5	28.79	108.0
Nov.	30.52	31.49	29.40	96.9	103.8	30.50	00.1	28.79	106.0
Dec.	29.64	32.17	30.19	92.1	98.2	30.50	97.2	28.79	103.0
Jan.	29.27	32.59	30.61	89.8	95.6	30.50	96.0	28.79	101.7
Feb.	29.15	32.55	30.56	89.6	95.4	30.26	96.3	28.79	101.3
Mar.	28.74	32.64	30.64	88.1	93.8	30.26	95.0	28.79	99.8
Apr.	29.91	32.97	30.97	90.7	96.6	30.38	98.5	28.79	103.9
May	9.97	32.85	30.88	91.2	97.1	30.26	99.0	28.79	104.1
June	30.13	32.76	30.89	92.0	97.5	30.13	100.0	28.79	104.7
July	30.08	32.09	30.24	93.7	99.5	30.13	99.8	28.79	104.5
Average 1949	30.41	32.15	30.04	94.6	101.2	30.50	99.7	28.79	105.6

Table 6.- Grade distribution of upland cotton crops, United States,
1948 and 1949

Grade	1949		1948		1949 as per-cent of 1948
	1,000 bales	Percent	1,000 bales	Percent	Percent
White & Extra White					
Good Middling and higher	49	0.3	111	0.8	44.1
Stict Middling	912	5.8	1,762	12.1	51.8
Middling	4,299	27.1	5,579	38.3	77.1
Strict Low Middling	5,252	33.0	3,578	24.5	146.8
Low Middling	1,757	11.1	1,031	7.1	170.4
Strict Good Ordinary	286	1.8	362	2.5	79.0
Good Ordinary	35	0.2	83	0.5	42.2
Spotted					
Good Middling	55	0.3	75	0.5	73.3
Strict Middling	804	5.1	617	4.2	130.3
Middling	1,349	8.5	493	3.4	273.6
Strict Low Middling	477	3.0	306	2.1	155.9
Low Middling	108	0.7	250	1.7	43.2
Tinged, all grades	97	0.6	176	1.2	55.1
Stained, all grades	1/	---	3	2/	---
Gray, all grades	398	2.5	106	0.7	375.5
Below Grade	19	0.1	45	0.3	42.2
Total	15,897	100.0	14,577	100.0	109.1

Compiled from reports of the Cotton Branch, PMA.

1/ Less than 500 bales.
2/ Less than 0.05 percent.

Table 7.- Cotton: Acreage harvested and ginnings, by
States, United States, 1947-49

State	Acreage harvested			Cotton ginned		
	1949 1/	1948	1947	1949 1/	1948	1947
	1,000 acres	1,000 acres	1,000 acres	1,000 running bales	1,000 running bales	1,000 running bales
Alabama ....:	1,810	1,630	1,500	853	1,167	907
Arizona ....:	373	281	225	549	322	235
Arkansas ....:	2,450	2,220	2,050	1,604	1,922	1,242
California ......:	957	804	534	1,285	974	766
Florida ....:	44	29	24	9	8	6
Georgia ....:	1,550	1,289	1,270	613	747	647
Louisiana ....:	1,060	950	830	633	733	490
Mississippi .....:	2,770	2,560	2,350	1,460	2,292	1,517
Missouri ....:...:	583	555	431	477	512	315
New Mexico ...,..:	310	209	151	263	225	170
North Carolina ..:	815	725	647	491	697	458
Oklahoma ....:	1,300	1,025	1,120	587	362	318
South Carolina ..:	1,270	1,120	1,050	566	872	642
Tennessee ....:	830	770	700	622	641	507
Texas ....:	10,725	8,610	8,350	5,860	3,063	3,314
Virginia ....:	32	26	23	18	21	15
Other States 2/..:	19	18	14	11	11	8
United States ...:	26,898	22,821	21,269	15,901	14,580	11,557

Compiled from reports of the Bureau of the Census and Bureau of Agriculture
Economics.

1/ Preliminary.
2/ Includes Illinois, Kansas, Kentucky, and Nevada.

Table 6.- Cotton: Average consumption per working day, United States, 1939-40 to date

Year beginning August	Aug. Running bales	Sept. Running bales	Oct. Running bales	Nov. Running bales	Dec. Running bales	Jan. Running bales	Feb. Running bales	Mar. Running bales	Apr. Running bales	May Running bales	June Running bales	July Running bales
1939	27,420	30,448	31,561	33,429	32,506	32,524	32,016	29,866	28,754	28,517	28,271	28,306
1940	29,586	31,133	33,514	36,155	37,023	37,548	39,671	40,703	4,861	42,954	41,705	42,263
1941	41,525	40,836	42,007	43,546	40,381	44,072	45,363	43,973	46,135	45,613	43,978	43,241
1942	44,044	44,639	44,740	44,533	42,540	44,721	44,716	43,366	43,340	44,015	41,747	39,994
1943	38,327	40,565	40,819	39,948	37,008	38,987	39,239	39,284	39,431	37,014	36,628	36,170
1944	36,589	38,518	36,505	38,904	37,940	37,797	39,713	38,974	37,214	36,907	37,426	32,046
1945	32,106	35,920	33,396	34,569	32,597	36,054	38,015	38,300	37,506	38,732	39,616	33,164
1946	38,989	39,886	40,592	42,830	36,969	42,222	41,969	41,681	40,109	37,541	34,734	30,808
1947	33,946	33,889	36,421	38,967	34,311	40,033	39,943	38,259	38,300	38,318	36,379	29,879
1948	33,130	34,363	33,567	31,901	29,368	3 , 00	32,546	31,364	28,955	26,999	27,302	22,721
1949	28,830	32,963	34,972	35,919	34,953	1/37,651	1/37,592					

Compiled from reports of the Bureau of the Census.
1/ Based on 4 weeks.

Table 9 .- umber of working days per m nth in cotton industry, United S tes, 1939-40 to date 1/

Year beginning August	August Days	September Days	October Days	November Days	December Days	January Days	February Days	Mch Days	April Days	May Days	June Days	July Days
939	23	20 1/2	21 3/4	21 1/2	20	22 1/2	20 2/3	21	21 2/3	22 1/2	20	22
940	22	20 1/2	23	20 1/2	21	22 1/2	20	21	22	21 1/2	21	22
94	21	21 1/2	22 3/4	19 1/2	22	21 1/2	19 2/3	22	21 2/3	21	22	23
1942	21	21 1/2	21 3/4	20 1/2	22	20 1/2	19 2/3	23	21 2/3	20 1/2	22	21
1943	22	21 1/2	20 3/4	21 1/2	23	21	20 2/3	23	19 2/3	22 1/2	22	20
1944	23	20 1/2	21 3/4	21 1/2	20	22 1/2	19 2/3	22	20 2/3	22 1/2	21	21
1945	23	19 1/2	22 3/4	21 1/2	20	22 1/2	19 2/3	21	21 2/3	22 1/2	20	22
1946	22	20 1/2	23	20 1/2	21	22 1/2	20	21	22	21 1/2	21	22
1947	21	21 1/2	22 3/4	19 1/2	22	21 1/2	19 2/3	23	21 2/3	20 1/2	22	21
948	22	21 1/2	20 3/4	21 1/2	23	21	19 2/3	23	20 2/3	21 1/2	22	20
949	23	21 1/2	20 3/4	21 1/2	21	2/19 1/2	2/19 2/3	3/25	2/19 2/3 3/20	2/19 2/3 2/20	24 1/2	19
950	2/20	3/24 1/2	2/19 3/4	3/24 1/2. 2/19	1/2. 2/19	2/19 1/2. 2/19	2/19 2/3.					

Compiled from reports of the Bureau of the Census.

1/ Calendar months through December 1949; 4 and 5 week eriods approximately coinciding with calendar months after that date. The number of working days is based on a 5-day week with the following allowances for holidays: January 1, 1/2 day; February 22, 1/3 day; April 19, 1/3 day; May 30, 1/2 day; July 4, full day; September 1/2 day; October 12, 1/4 day; November 1/2 day; December 25, full day. No deduction is made for holidays falling on Saturday.
2/ 4 weeks.
3/ 5 eks.

Table 10.- Cotton: "Exports from the United States to specified countries,
August-January, average 1935-39, 1940-44, and 1946-49

ntry of tination	Year beginning August 1					
	Average 1935-39	Average 1940-44	1946 1/	1947 1/	1948 2/	1949 3/
	1,000 running bales	1,000 running bales	1,000 running bales	1,000 running bales	1,000 running bales	1,000 running bales
Europe						
ited Kingdom ...:	896.8	337.6	180.1	159.8	228.5	322.7
istria ....:	.1	0	3.5	0	16.7	19.9
lgium and Lux. .:	112.0	0	104.7	35.2	76.2	93.5
echoslovakia ...:	34.6	0	74.0	0	.4	35.4
nmark ....:	19.6	0	0.	.0	14.0	16.0
re ....:	0	0	.1	0	.8	1.6
tonia ....:	5.9	0	0.	0	0	0
nland ....:	22.8	1.8	21.7	10.6	18.3	3.1
ance ....:	486.8	2.0	152.6	74.7	236.6	470.0
rmany ..,......:	328.6	0	127.8	51.3	265.9	328.6
braltar ....:	0	0	.1	0	0	0
eece ....:	0.8	0.1	9.7	1.0	1 9	15.5
ngary ....:	3.1	0	0.	0	1 7	18.1
aly ....:	246.4	0	261.7	20.9	304.8	313.9
tvia ....:	4.2	0	0.	0	0	0
therlands .....:	76.2	0	75.9	23.2	84.0	126.8
rway ....:	11.4	0	3.3	1.5	7.2	4.4
land and Danzig.:	105.4	0	3.7	14.6	54.4	26.4
ortugal ....:	22.8	.1	0	0	0	0
pain ....:	65.2	45.8	29.4	0	11.0	26.6
weden ....:	79.4	5.6	14.7	4.7	.4	6.9
witzerland ....:	7.1	.1	9.1	1.8	29.0	30.2
.S.S.R. ....:	0	27.8	0	0	0	0
ugoslavia ......:	11.7	0	60.1	0	17.5	11.1
ther Europe ...:	2.3	0	0	0	3.4	1.6
otal Europe ...:	2,543.2	420.9	1,132.2	399.3	1,372.7	1,812.3
Other Countries						
anada ....:	161.8	153.2	157.1	84.5	134.4	130.7
exico ....:	0	0	0.	4/	0	0
uba ....:	7.0	3.9	12.4	9.2	.9	11.8
olombia ....:	10.3	1.9	1.0	0	20.0	19.9
dia ....:	38.6	.1	0	0	2.4	6.5
ina ....:	71.6	4.	97.3	6.8	92.9	17.4
pan ....:	662.8	11.	446.0	364.6	203.6	311.5
ng Kong ....:	0		1.7	0	2.9	28.2
stralia ....:	.4.5	7.	5.9	10.0	0	0
lestine ....:	0		.2	.5	4.7	3 6
ench Indo China :	11.6	2.	5.	4.0	4.1	5 3
rea ....:	0			23.0	0	8.5
her countries ..:	15.0	80.6	6.6	0	46.8	57.2
rld total .....:	3,526.4	685.5	1,865.7	901.9	1,884.5	2,412.9

mpiled from reports of the Bureau of the Census.
/ Excludes War Department shipments. 2/ Includes Army Civilian Supply Exports.
/ Preliminary. 4/ Less than 50 bales.

Table 11.- ECA purchase authorizations issued to April 1, 1950 for cotton
to be exported during fiscal year 1949-50, and actual exports,
United States, July 1949 and August-February, 1949-50

Country	Authorizations for shipment of cotton during fiscal year, 1949-50		Exports from United States	
			July, 1949	August-February 19
	1,000 dollars	1,000 bales 1/	1,000 running bales	1,000 running bales
Austria ....:	9,725	61.3	.8	20.6
Belgium ....:	2/ 6,000	2/ 37.5	8.0	113.5
Denmark ....:	4,794	30.2	1.0	20.0
France ....:	123,900	780.5	21.6	509.2
French North Africa .:	1,328	8.4	0	3.4
Germany ....:	145,708	917.8	32.6	367.9
Greece ....:	10,078	63.5	2.0	18.8
Italy ....:	113,219	713.2	12.2	397.1
Netherlands ....:	38,545	242.8	3.8	144.9
Norway.............:	2,200	13.9	1.1	4.9
Sweden ....:	2,100	13.2	0	10.7
United Kingdom ....:	97,500	614.2	24.6	403.8
Korea ....:	10,370	65.3	1.1	16.1
Total ....:	2/565,467	2/3,562.0	108.8	2,030.9

Compiled from reports of ECA and Bureau of the Census.

1/ Calculated at $158.75 per bale.
2/ Does not include 3.0 million dollars authorized in March, 1950, for procureme
of about 19,500 bales to be exported after July 20, 1950.

Table 12.- ...e of ginnings, of carry-over and of CC stocks from 1948 upland cotton crop and grade of ginnings and of CCC loans from the 1949 upland cotton crop

| | 1948 crop cotton | | | 1949 crop cotton | | | |
	Ginnings	Carry-over Aug. 1, 1949	CC Aug. 1, 1949	Ginnings through Jan. 15, 1950	Percent	CC loans as of Jan. 31, 1950	Percent
	1,000 bales	1,000 bales	1,000 bales	1,000 bales		1,000 bales	Percent
White							
Gd Middling and higher	110	40	30	48	0.3	4	0.2
Strict Middling	1,762	66	469	911	5.8	74	3.5
Middling	5,579	1,999	1,391	4,291	27.5	432	20.5
St Lw Middling	3,578	1,420	1,137	5,228	33.6	890	42.1
Low Middling	1,032	457	338	1,716	11.0	97	4.6
Strict Good Ordinary	362	102	58	242	1.5	4	0.2
Good Ordinary	83	18	9	21	0.1	2/	3/
Gd							
Gd Middling	75	8	7	54	0.3	5	0.2
St Middling	617	106	85	800	5.1	144	6.8
Middling	493	150	110	1,335	8.5	411	19.5
St Low Middling	307	108	79	435	2.8	10	0.5
Low Middling	250	66	40	77	0.5	2/	3/
Tinged and Stained	179	50	27	77	0.5	1	3/
Gray	106	41	36	394	2.5	43	2.0
Below	45	3	0	7	3/	---	---
Total 4/	14,577	5,216	5/3,794	15,638	100.0	2,114	100.0

Compiled from reports of the Cotton Branch, and ...tion and Marketing Administration. 1/ Ginnings ...re preliminary. ...on CC loans do not include Cotton Cooperative Associations cotton of ...t 700,000 bales, for which grade distribution ...s not available. 2/ Less than 500 bales. 3/ Less than 0.05 percent. 4/ ...als ...re ...ore figures rounded. 5/ Data by ...s preliminary, total revised.

Av 1920-29	563 3	52.1	79 5	1/	9 6	59.3	76.4	2 4	10.5	5 2	.2	1	2/	22.6	.2	245.4
1930	416 3	58.3	48 6	4/	10.0	40 9	64.4	5.9	8.0	8.8	.4	5/	5/	20.0	1.5	149.5
1931	367 0	37.1	61.6	5/	8 5	44 7	54.3	2 8	7.8	5.8	.2	5/	0.	14.7	.8	128,8.
19 2	375.4	6 7	116.7	4/	5 9	47 4	50.2	1.4	5.6	0	.1	5/	5/	19.3	1 0	100,9
19 3	302 0	17 1	88 1	4/	1 7	44 4	45.1	.5	4.9	.1		5/	5/	13.1	.2	86.7
19 4	226 3	12.5	47 9	4/	1 2	33 5	67.6	2 1	3 4		.2	5/	5/	2.6	.1	54.9
19 5	185 6	12 0	47 1	4/	.9	21 4	55.4	.5	2.2		.1	5/	5/	4.9	.1	40 6
19 6	200.5	16.2	41 5	4/	1 0	21 3	59 7	.3	2 1	.3	.1	5/	5/	10.6	1	47 3
19 7	236.3	20.4	66.7	4/	1 8	17.7	65 8	1 6	3 1		2/	5/	5/	9 2	2	49 3
19 8	319.6	25 5	125.5	4/	2 4	36.8	48 4	1 1	4 1	1 1	2/	5/	5/	15 2	.5	59.0 .
19 9	367.5	43 5	107 5	2/	3 6	45.8	63.4	4.3	8 1	1.	2/	5/	.1	19.4	.9	69.8
Av. 1930-39	299.7	26.9'	75 1	2/	3.7	35 4	57 4	2 1	4.9	1.9	.1	2/	2/	12.9	.5	78.8
1940	357.9	91 7	74.2	5/	25 8	36.9	44 3	11.3	5 2	3.6	5/	5/	2/	15.7	1.2	58.0
1941	586.7	115 7	88.3	2/	6 5	51.3	62 0	48.9	12.7	1.5	2/	5/	5/	17.6	.7	151.5
1942	447.8	174 2	0	.2	7 8	34.4	47 7	6.8	12.3	1.9	5/	5/	5/	13.1	.1	149,3
1943	538.5	189.4	0	5/	13.6	25.1	27.9	0	11 5	31.5	2/	0	7.8	12.6	0	219.1
1944	638 1	218 7	0	5/	19.6	26 3	31 2	0	9 7	3.3	5.2	0	7.5	15.1	0	301 5
1945	672.8	191.1	2.5	4.9	29 1	19 6	32 4	4.2	6 0	7.7	11.8	2/	13 8	11.9	0	337 8
1946	774 9	203 0	85.2	4 2	26 8	23.2	33 5	70.7	10.7	.5	6.9	.3	10.8	11 0.	7.9	280.2
1947	1,474 8	285 3	90.8	10.1	94 1	56 3	43.4	33 2	27.4	42.1	17.6	6.2	30.7	19 9	46.6	670.1
1948	940.4	160.4	83.0	40.4	98 0	49.9	39 8	17 9	38 9	26.9	23.3	4.4	26.3	9.6	10 .0	125.6
1949	880 2	173 7	112.7	109.2	54.8	44 9	44 2	38.3	28 2	23.2	21 3	19.0	18.1	15.0	1 7	166.9
Av 1940-49	731.2	180.3	53.7	16 9	39 6	36 7	40.6	23 1	16.3	14.2	8.6	3.0	11.5	14.2	17 4	255.1

			Percentage each country is of total exports												
	:Percent	Percent	Percent	Percent	Percent	Percent	Percent	Percent	Percent	Percent	Percent	Percent	Percent	Percent	Percent	Percent
1920	100 0	8.1	7 7	4/	0.2	7 1	19.6	0.8	4.4	0.6	4/	6/	6/	2 7	4/	48.8
1921	100.0	7 8	9 7	5/	8	13 1	4 1	.2	.4	.5	5/	5/	6/	3.8	5/	59.5
1922	100,0	8.5	15.9	5/	1.1	10 6	8.3		8	.7	5/	6/	6/	3.8	5/	50.1
1923	100 0	7.6	15.9	5/	1 5	11 2	18.7	5/	1 2	.4	6/	6/	6/	4 8	5/	38.5
1924	100.0	7.0	14 1	5/	1 6	13.1	16 9	5/	-2 2	.5	6/	6/	6/	4 9	5/	39.6
1925	100 0	7 0	14.7	5/	2 2	11 6	12.2	5/	1 9	.8	6/	6/	6/	5.7	0.3	4 7
1926	100 0	9 0	19 7	5/	2 7	10 3	13 6	5/	1.7	.7:	6/	6/	6/	3.4	1	3 .6
1927	100 0	11 2	15.6	5/	2 7	10.7	14 8	4	1 1	1.4	6/	6/	6/	4 8	.4	37.6,
1928	100 0	12 7	17.2	5/	2 5	9.1	12 9	.8	1.6	1.7	6/	6/	6/	4 6	.4	36.5
1929	100 0	13 3.	14 4	5/	2 4	10.7	13.6	1.5	2.1	1.9	6/	6/	6/	2 6	.6	36.8,
Av. 1920-29	100.0	9.2	14 1	4/	1 7	10 5	13.6	4	1 9	9	6/	6/	6/	4 0	6/	43.5
1930	100 0	14 0	11.7	4/	2 4	9 8	15 5	1 4	1 9	2.1	0.1	6/	6/	4.8	.4	36.8
1931	100,0	10 1	16.8	5/	2 3	12.2	14 8	8	-.1	1.5	.1	6/	6/	4 0	2	35 1
1932	100 0	7 1	31.1	5/	.5	12 6	13 4	4	1.5	6/	6/	6/	6/	5.1	3	26 9
1933	100 0	5.7	29 2	5/	.6	14 7	14 9	2	1.6	6/	6/	6/	6/	4.3	.1	28.7
1934	100 0	5.5	21 2	5/	5	14 8	29.9	9	1.5	.2	6/	6/	6/	1.1	1	24.3
1935	100 0	6.5	25.4	5/	5	11 5	29 8	.3	1 2	.2	6/	6/	0.1	2 6	1 1	21 9
1936	100,0	8 1,	20.7	6/	5	10 6	29.8	.2	1 0	.1	.1	6/	6/	5 3	.1	2 6
1937	100 0	8.6,	28.2	7	8	7.5	27 8	.7	1 3	.2	6/	6/	6/	3 9	1 1	20 9
1938	100 0	8 0	39 2	6/	8	11.5	15 1	.3	.3	.3	6/	6/	6/	4 8	.2	18.5
1939	100.0	11 8	29 3	6/	1.0	12 5	17 3	1.2	2 2	.3	6/	6/	6/	5 3	.2	19.0
Av 1930-39	100,0	9.0'	25.1	6/	1 2	11.8	19 2	7	1 6	.6	6/	6/	6/	4 3	2	26.3
1940	100 0	25.6	20 7	6/	4 4	10 3	12.4	3 2	1 4	1 0	6/	6/	6/	4.4	0.3	16 2
1941	100 0	19 7	15.1	6/	6 2	8.7	10 6	8.3	2 2	.3	6/	6/	6/	3 0		25.8
1942	100 0	38.9	0	6/	1 7	7.7.	10 7	1 5	2.7	.4	6/	6/	6/	2 9	6/	33 3
1943	100 0	35 2	0	6/	2.5	4.7	5.2	0	2 1	5.8	6/	0	1.4	2 3	0	40.7
1944	100 0	34 3	0	6/	3.1	4.1	4 9	0	1.5	.5	.8	0	1.2	2 4	0	47 3
1945	100 0	28 4:	0.4	0.7	4 3	2 9	4.8	.6	.8	1.1	1.8	6/	2.1	1 8	0	50 2
1946	100 0	26 2'	11 0	5	3 5	3 0	4 3	9 1	1 4	6/	.9	6/	1.4	1.4	1 2	36 1
1947	100,0	19 3	6.2	7	6 4	3 8	2.9	2 3	1 9	2.9	1.2	0.4	2.1	1 4	3.2	45.3
1948	100 0	17.2	8 8	4 3	10 4	5.3	4.2	1 9	4 1	2 9	2.5	.5	2.8	1 0	11 2	22 9
1949	100 0	19.7	12.8	12 4	6.2	5 1	5.0	4 4	3 2	2.6	2.4	2.2	2.1	1 7	1.2	19.0
Av 1940-49	200 0	24.7.	7.3	2.3	5.4	5.0	5.6	3.2	2 2	1.9	1.2	.4	1.6	1.9	2.4	34.9

Compiled from reports of the Bureau of the Census.
1/ Includes duck, tire fabrics, all other cotton cloths, bleached, unbleached, yarn dyed and colored, and mixtures made largely of cotton yarns.
2/ Totals and averages were made before figures were rounded to millions.
3/ Linear yards.
4/ If any included in other countries.
5/ Less than 50,000 yards.
6/ Less than 0.05 percent.

Table 14 - Exports of cotton cloths by country of destination, United States, 1937 and 1947-49 1/

Country of destination	1949 2/		1948		1947		1939			Country of destination	1949 2/		1948		1947		1939	
	Million sq. yds.	Per-cent	Million sq. yds.	Per-cent	Million sq. yds.	Per-cent	Million sq. yds.	Per-cent			Million sq. yds.	Per-cent	Million sq. yds.	Per-cent	Million sq. yds.	Per-cent	Million sq. yds.	Per-cent
World total 3/	880.2	100.0	940.4	100.0	1,474.8	100.0	367.5	100.0	::	Asia, total 3/	357.5	40.6	311.9	33.2	358.0	24.3	119.0	32.4
America, total 3/	180.1	20.4	169.8	18.1	287.3	19.5	48.8	13.3	::	Aden	2/	4/	5	0.1	6	4/	8	4
Canada	173.7	19.7	160.4	17.1	278.3	18.9	43.5	11.8	::	Afghanistan	1.4	0.2	1	0.1	1	4/	1	0
Greenland	0	0	0	0	.4	4/	0	0	::	Arabia	1	4/				4/	0	0
Mexico	5.7	0.6	8.2	0.9	6.9	0.5	3.8	1.0	::	Bahrein	2	0.1	1	0	2	4/	0	0
Newfoundland	7	1	12	0.1	1.6	0.1	15	0.4	::	British Malaya	10	1.2	106	11.3	47	3.2	.9	.2
America, total 3/	44.9	5.1	49.9	5.3	56.3	3.8	45.8	12.5	::	Ceylon	21.3	2.4	23.	2.5	18	1.2	2/	4/
British Honduras	.4	4/	1.1	0.1	1.1	0.1	5	0.1	::	China	2/	4/		3/	1	3	1.4	0.4
Canal Zone	.4	4/	.5	4/			1	4	::									
Costa Rica	8.6	1.0	7.1	0.8	8	.6	4.1	1	::	French Indo China	2/	4/	.7	0.1	35	2.4	1.2	0.3
El Salvador		0	14.6	1.8	13	9	12.9	5	::	Hong Kong	4.5	0.5	1.1	0.1	3	0.3	1.3	0.4
Guatemala	1		7.7	.8	9	.6	2/	4/	::	India	3		3.2	3	9.	0	4	0
Honduras	1		5.4	0	10	7	4.1	1	::	Indonesia	38.3	4.4	17.9	9	33	2	4.3	1
Nicaragua	0		8.5	0	6	4	12.0	3	::	Iran	109.2	12.4	40.4	3	10	0	2/	4/
Panama Republic	0		5.1	0	5	4	2.5	7	::	Iraq	7.2	0	6.5	7	4	0	8	0
Others			0		0	0	9.3	5	::	Israel and Pales.	3.9	0	.5	4/	3	0		
									::	Japan	.3	4/	2/	4/	2/	4/		
Bermuda and Carib.									::	Korea	.4	4/	.3	4/	2/	4/		
Sea, total 3/	78.3	8.9	72.1	7.7	110.3	7.5	101.4	27.6	::	Kuwait	.7	0.1	.7	0.1	1.3	0.1		
Bahamas	.5	.1	.3	4/	.9	0.1	0	0	::	Lebanon	1.8	0.2	2.8	0.3	2/	4/		
Barbadoes	.6	.1		4/	1.4	.1	5	0.1	::	Neth E Indies								
Bermuda	.2	4/	7	1	4	4/	1	4/	::	(see Indonesia)								
Cuba	44.2	5.2	39.	4.2	43	3.0	63.4	17.3	::	Pakistan	14.8	1.6	42	0.4	5/	4/	0	0
Curacao	1.7		2	0.2	1	.1	0	0	::	Philippine Rep	112.	12.8	83.0	8.8	96.9	6.6	107	29
Dominican R' p	10	1	11	1.2	15.	.0	5.5	1.5	::	Portuguese Asia			.3	4/	2/	4/		
French W. I	1				2	1	2/	4/	::	Saudi Arabia	4.	0.	9.1	1.0	9.6	0.7		
Haiti	15	1.	9	1.0	19	.3	19	5.3	::	Siam (see Thailand)								
Jamaica	.1	4/	3	4/	14	.0	8.5	2.3	::	Syria	.4	4/	1.3	0.1	11.4	0.8	2/	4/
Leeward Islands	2.0	.2	3	0.3	3	3	0	0	::	Thailand	19.0	2.2	4.0	0.4	6.2	.4	3	0
Trinidad and									::	Trans Jordan	.9	0.1	.9	0.	5/	4/		
Tobago	2.0	.8	4	0.4	7.8	0.5	1.7	0.5	::	Turkey	4.4	.5	1.5	0.	30.8	2.1	2	0
Others	0	0			0	0	6	0.6	::	Others	0	0	0.1	4/	5/	4/		
America, total 3/	66.9	7.6	89.0	9.5	133.9	9.1	41.5	11.3	::	Australia and Oceania, total 3/	6.5	0.7	15.1	1.6	77.8	2.3	1.5	0.4
Argentina	2.0	.2	15.6	1.7	58.7	4.0	2/	4/	::	Australia	4.2	0.6	11.1	1.2	67.0	4.5	1.1	0.3
Bolivia	6.7	.8	4.1	0.4	2.7	0.2	.1	4/	::	British Western								
Brazil			7	1	8	1	.7	0.2	::	Pacific Islands	2/	4/	.1	4/	1.5	4/	2/	4/
British Guiana	1	.1	8.4	8.1	1	1	.7	0.2	::	French Oceanic	1.6	0.2	.7	0.1	1.5	0/	2/	4/
Chile	4	0.4	8.2	2	9	6	6.7	1.8	::	New Guinea	2/	4/	2.9	0.3	5/	4/	2/	4/
Colombia	8	0.8	1.7	1	6	3.6	23	6.4	::	New Zealand	7	0.1	0	3	7.6	.5	.3	4/
Ecuador	.7	.6	7	4	4	.3	8	0.2	::	Others	0	0	.3	4/	1.2	1	.1	4/
French Guinea	.4	.1	4/	.1	5	.3	2/	4/	::									
Paraguay	3.5	0.4	2	4/	1	0.1	2/	4/	::	Africa, total 3/	103.1	11.7	185.2	19.7	310.6	21.1	4.1	1.1
Peru	6.6	0.7	2.4	0.3	4	.3	.5	0.1	::	Algeria	2/	4/	1.9	0.2	4.8	0.3	2/	4/
Surinam	2.4	.2	4	0.4	4	.3	3	.1	::	Anglo Egy. Sudan	2/	4/	.7	0.1	3.1	0.2	2/	4/
Uruguay	.9	.1	5	0.2	8	.5	1	4/	::	Angola	.5	0.1	4/	4/	2/	4/	2/	4/
Venezuela	28.2	3.2	3	9	4.1	27	.8	8.1	2.2	::	Belgian Congo	18.1	2.1	26.3	2.	30.7	2.	.1	4/
Others	0	1	4/	2	4/	0	0	0	0	::	British E Africa	.3	0.1	6.8	0.7	39.7	2.7	2/	4/
Europe, total 3/	42.9	4.9	47.5	5.1	140.6	9.5	5.1	1.4	::	British W Africa	.2	4/	.6	4/	9.5	0/	2/	4/
Albania	0	0	0	0	.1	4/	0	0	::	Cameroons	1	0	1.2	0.1	5.7	0.4	2/	4/
Austria	.3	4/	2/	4/	.1	4/	2/	4/	::	Egypt	2/	4/	2/	4/	2.0	0.1	.1	4/
Czechoslovakia	2.5	.3	3.9	0.4	9	0.6	.1	4/	::	Ethiopia	3.5	0.4	8.6	0.9	11.4	0.8	0	0
Denmark	.9	0	1	2/	4/	2/	4/	::	French Eq Africa	1.2	0.1	2.8	.3	5.0	0.3	2/	4/
Ireland	.1	2	0.8	0.3	19.9	1.3	2/	4/	::	French Morocco	11.7	1.3	7.5	.8	5.9	0.4	2/	4/
France	1.2	.8	4.5	0.5	2/	4/	2/	4/	::	French Somaliland	2	4/	.8	.6	2/	4/	2/	4/
Germany	7	.1	4/	.1	4/	2/	4/	::	French W. Africa	5.6	0.6	7.8	.8	25.9	1.8	0	0
Greece	1.1	.1	.3	4/	1.8	0.1	2/	4/	::	Gold Coast	0	0	.1	.1	11.0	0.8	2/	4/
Iceland	1.0	.1	7	0	.8	0.1	2/	4/	::	Liberia	1.9	0.2	.0	.2	8.4	0.	2/	4/
Italy	2/	4/	.3	4/	2	1	2/	4/	::	Madagascar	1.0	0.1	.3	0.7	8.6	0.	2/	4/
Netherlands	.6	.1	1.1	0.1	2.6	2	.1	0.1	::	Madeira Islands	2/	0.1	.1	.3	2/	4/	2/	4/
Norway	5.2	0.6	28.9	0.4	18.7	3	0	0	::	Mozambique	.2	0.1	1.0	0.1	4.7	0.3	2/	4/
Portugal	.1	4/	2/	4/	.5	4/	2/	4/	::	Nigeria	.2	4/	7.4	0.8	34.4	2.3	0	0
Sweden	1.1	.1	.3	0.2	29.0	2.0	2.1	0.6	::	Northern Rhodesia	2/	4/	.4	4/	.2	4/	2/	4/
Switzerland	.3		7	.8	2.0	0.1	1.1	0.3	::	Southern Rhodesia	2/	4/	2.0	0.2	9.4	0.6	2/	4/
United Kingdom	23.2	2.6	9	0	42.0	9	.1	4/	::	Tangier	1.0	1.0	.8	4/	.8	4/	2/	4/
U.S.S.R.	1	4/	3	4/	0	0	0	0	::	Tunisia	0	0	.2	4/	.3	4/	2/	4/
Yugoslavia	1	0	2/	4/	2/	4/	0	0	::	Union of S. Africa	54.8	6.2	98.0	10.4	94.1	6.4	3.6	1.0
Others	0	0	0.2	4/	8.3	0.6	1.3	0.4	::	Others	.3	4/	.3	4/	9.2	0.6	.4	0.1

Compiled from reports of the Bureau of the Census.
Includes duck, tire fabrics, all other cotton cloths bleached, unbleached, yarn dyed and colored, and mixtures made largely of cotton yards. 2/ Preliminary.
All totals were made before data were rounded. 4/ Less than 0.05 percent. 2/ Less than 50,000 yards.

average	:	24.5	24.4	30.4	27.8	26.4	25.0	24.9	22.3	22.0	24.8	23.5	23.7	299.7
	:													
1940	:	33.9	34.1	35.9	35.5	29.9	24.8	26.8	25.0	24.6	28.1	30.8	28.5	357.9
1941	:	35.7	34.7	40.2	39.2	46.9	39.6	41.5	51.3	47.3	77.8	63.6	4/ 69.0	586.7
1942	:	47.5	50.2	36.0	31.8	29.3	25.6	29.1	48.1	29.7	36.4	35.7	4/ 48.4	447.8
1943	:	42.3	37.5	51.8	44.8	49.7	40.0	40.1	48.9	51.4	39.0	49.2	4/ 43.8	538.5
1944	:	34.2	42.0	46.0	43.3	48.7	51.6	63.2	63.4	58.8	55.0	77.2	4/ 54.6	638.1
1945	:	51.8	51.7	59.0	52.8	51.4	56.7	62.9	57.0	58.0	49.0	68.8	4/ 52.8	672.8
1946	:	62.8	66.2	71.5	65.2	73.1	68.3	57.5	59.9	41.6	42.6	70.3	4/101.3	774.9
1947	:	89.0	88.1	126.5	138.2	146.7	125.2	129.3	140.7	130.7	135.3	122.7	4/102.4	1,474.8
1948	:	93.9	82.4	75.6	80.1	79.9	73.1	71.9	63.7	62.5	83.3	58.0	116.0	940.4
1949	:	102.3	88.2	93.5	79.4	74.3	81.1	65.9	60.0	66.4	60.4	52.8	55.9	880.2
10-year	:													
average	:	59.3	57.5	63.6	61.0	63.0	58.6	58.8	61.8	57.1	60.7	62.9	67.3	731.2
	:													
1950	:	36.5												

Compiled from Monthly Summary of Foreign Commerce of the United States, and reports of the Bureau of the Census.
1/ Includes duck, tire fabrics, all other cotton cloths, bleached, unbleached, yarn dyed and colored, and mixtures made largely of cotton yarns.
2/ Totals were made before figures were rounded to millions, and are not always summation of monthly data owing to revisions and adjustments.
3/ Linear yards.
4/ Arbitrary adjustments to calendar year totals.

Table 16.- Cotton: Exports from the United States, February, 1949 and 1950

Country of destination	February 1950 Pima and Sea Island	1-1/8" and over	1-1/16" to 1-1/8"	15/16" to 1-1/16"	Under 15/16"	Total	1949 Total
	Running bales	Running bales	Running bales	Running bales	Running bales	Running bales	Running bales
Europe							
Austria ....:	---	22	701	---	723	8,358	
Belgium and Lux..:	725	6,852	8,222	4,207	20,006	17,229	
Czechoslovakia ..:	---	1,281	2,705	---	3,986	22,362	
Denmark ....:	---	---	3,966	---	3,966	3,450	
Finland ....:	---	---	---	---	---	3,090	
France ....:	6,187	10,019	81,152	1,826	99,184	78,137	
Germany ....:	4,799	19,243	15,197	60	39,299	22,279	
Greece ....:	806	591	1,881	---	3,278	544	
Hungary ....:	---	21	800	---	821	0	
Ireland ....:	500	---	50	333	883	400	
Italy............:	1,775	26,129	47,786	7,462	83,152	47,239	
Netherlands .....:	5,866	4,984	7,203	---	18,053	6,840	
Norway ....:	---	200	220	---	420	800	
Poland and Danzig:	---	---	500	---	500	3,157	
Portugal.........:	---	---	---	---	---	100	
Rumania ....:	---	---	---	---	---	5,798	
Spain ....:	---	75	6,879	---	6,954	14,591	
Sweden ....:	---	25	3,821	---	3,846	0	
Switzerland .....:	650	100	455	50	1,255	2,471	
Trieste ....:	---	208	---	---	208	350	
United Kingdom ..:	6,216	21,006	46,922	6,889	81,033	103,978	
Yugoslovia ......:	500	4,900	400	---	5,800	6,096	
Total Europe ..:	28,024	95,656	228,860	20,827	373,367	347,269	
America							
Bolivia ....:	---	---	---	---	---	900	
Canada ....:	295	2,751	15,790	1,850	20,686	34,521	
Colombia ....:	401	3,117	31	---	3,549	3,558	
Chile ....:	108	---	---	43	151	3,650	
Cuba ....:	---	550	950	---	1,500	1,200	
Dominican Republic:	---	---	---	---	0	30	
Uruguay ....:	---	---	2	---	2	200	
Others							
China ....:	300	6,748	15,364	23,057	45,469	24,109	
Japan ....:	---	5,151	52,901	43,950	102,002	57,423	
India ....:	52,690	20,286	1,939	1,250	76,165	0	
Hong Kong ....:	402	400	2,324	19,207	22,333	7,185	
Taiwan (Formosa).:	407	---	---	72	479	0	
Palestine ....:	---	614	---	100	714	523	
Korea ....:	---	593	223	6,740	7,556	12,952	
Philippine Rep..:	---	---	600	---	600	700	
French Morocco ..:	---	---	162	---	162	427	
U. of S. Africa .:	---	---	213	---	213	932	
Netherlands Indies:	---	---	---	---	0	1,000	
Ethiopia ....:	---	---	---	---	0	500	
Total ....:	0	82,627	135,866	319,359	117,096	654,948	497,075

Compiled from reports of the Bureau of the Census.

Table 17.— Export of cotton linters from the United States,
January-February, 1950

Country of destination	January 1950	February, 1950		
		Grade 1-4	Grade 5-7	Total
	Bales	Bales	Bales	Bales
Europe				
France ....:	70	103	---	103
Germany ....:	29,199	-----	826	826
United Kingdom ....:	3,950	----	6,374	6,374
Total Europe ....:	33,219	103	7,200	7,303
America				
Canada ....:	2,449	2,146	75	2,221
Cuba ....:	15	----	----	----
Honduras.............:	5	---	----	----
Others				
Japan ....:	358	----	----	----
Union of South Africa.:	123	----	116	116
Total ....:	36,169	2,249	7,391	9,640

Compiled from reports of the Bureau of the Census.

Table 18.— Value of planned imports of raw cotton and total imports
of ECA participating countries, 1948 to 1951-52

Year	Raw cotton			Total imports		
	Gold and dollars 2/	Other currencies	Total	Gold and dollars 2/	Other currencies	Total
1948	313	564	877	6,337	15,259	21,596
1949-50	491	516	1,007	4,892	15,317	20,209
1950-51	507	580	1,087	4,266	15,531	19,797
1951-52	491	612	1,103	3,741	16,167	19,908

Organization for European Economic Co-operation. Second Report of the
O.E.E.C. European Recovery Programme published in Paris, February 1950,
chapter eleven, page 107.

1/ Metropolitan areas excluding Switzerland.
2/ The values in the gold and dollars column include all imports from
the United States and Canada and exclude dollar imports from other participating countries or their Overseas Territories. These are included
in the "other currencies" column which also includes the value of each
country's imports from its own Overseas Territories and from other par-
ticipants and their Overseas Territories.

U. S. Department of Agriculture
Washington 25, D. C.

OFFICIAL BUSINESS

BAE-CS-127-4/12/50- 2900
Permit No. 1001

Penalty for private use to avoid
payment of postage $300

Lightning Source UK Ltd.
Milton Keynes UK
UKHW021006161218
334046UK00008B/798/P